THE CHANGING FACES OF

Eynsham

BOOK ONE

Martin J. Harris

Robert Boyd
PUBLICATIONS

Published by
Robert Boyd Publications
260 Colwell Drive
Witney, Oxfordshire OX8 7LW

First published 1997

Copyright © Martin J. Harris and
Robert Boyd Publications

ISBN: 1 899536 18 3

OTHER TITLES IN THE
CHANGING FACES SERIES

Anyone can publish a book — why not you!

Have you ever wanted to publish a book? It is not as difficult as you might think. The publisher of this book provides a service to individuals and organisations large and small.

Advice can be given on all facets of production: typesetting, layout and design, paper stocks, styles of binding including wired, perfect, sewn, limp and cased binding, the options are almost endless. If you have a project you would like to discuss why not contact:

Robert Boyd
PRINTING & PUBLISHING SERVICES
260 Colwell Drive
Witney, Oxfordshire OX8 7LW

Printed and bound in Great Britain at The Alden Press, Oxford

Contents

Cover Illustrations

Front: Eynsham character and keen photographer Jim Evans (1897—1987) playing the drums outside his house in Mill Street. (Photograph taken in 1980 by Sue Chapman.) This book commemorates the centenary of his birth.

Back: The Square in Eynsham.

Acknowledgements

I would like to thank the following people who have been so kind in loaning photographs to me as well as providing me with much information about Eynsham: Brian Atkins, Geoff Batts, Clara and the late Reg Bloyce, Janet Brown, Don and Sue Chapman, Boycott Evans, David and Maggie Faulkner, Ron and Connie Gardner, Ron and Gladys Garner, Mona Gascoigne, Stanley Green, Harry Hardwick, Diane Harris, June Harris, Temperance Hawtin, Anita Holmes, Mary Oakeley, Mons Perkins, Andy and Phillis Pimm (who have spent many hours helping me out), Dorothy Porter, Harold and Veronica Quainton, Joyce Reeves, Donald and Pamela Richards, Grace Sloane, Ted and Hilda Sumner, Dave Tuckey, Bob and Vi Warren, Eric and Iris Wastie, Frankie Wastie, Kathleen Wastie, Joan Weedon, Ted Whelan, Terry Woodman, Anne Wrapson. The part of the Henry Taunt photograph shown on page 75 is courtesy of Oxfordshire Photographic Archive, Oxfordshire County Council which has many further excellent photographs that can be seen at the Centre for Oxfordshire Studies in the Central Library, Oxford. The professional photographer Sue Chapman (whose photographs are designated [SC] in this book) deserves a special mention for her excellent pictures of Eynsham that she has taken since she and husband Don came to live in Eynsham almost 30 years ago.

The following have also helped with details and encouragement: Roy Boulting, Jean Buttrick, Sylvia Chambers, Kenneth Cope, Ann Cross, Crown Prints for turning some slides into wonderful photographs, Vera Davies, Eynsham History Group, Cate Foster, Jack Green, John Hanson, Francis and E Margaret Harris, Tom Harris, Mike and Jenny Howard, Bryan and Julie Hyde, Sandra Jones and all at the Day Centre, Alison Lynn, Rowland and Diana Oakeley, Max and Joanna Peterson, Moyra Philcox, Ann Porter, John Richards, George and Maureen Roberts, Basil and Cis Seeney, Gary Walker and Ian Gaisford (the Botley barbers), Ian White of Premier and Nicky, Ken and Gill Williams, Sandra Wright, and Geoff Parkinson for his help with the layout of the book.

May I also thank any others whose names have been inadvertently omitted and apologise for any unintentional errors and misleading information that are subsequently discovered.

A note regarding the quality of the photographs. Please note that the quality of the photographs included in this book will vary, but where the photograph is of a poor standard it has been included for historical reasons or to make a valid point. I hope that this will not effect the enjoyment of the book.

Preface

I always enjoy books of old and new photographs of villages, towns and cities. For quite a few years I have wished that there would be such a book on Eynsham. Recently, Gladys Garner, daughter of the late Jim Evans who took many photographs during his life, encouraged me to carry out such a project. Helen Peacocke, a journalist for the Oxford Mail and Times and an Eynsham resident, also gave me the confidence that I could produce a book. Now, thanks to Robert Boyd Publications, this has been made possible. And I hope that the information included makes it more than just a book of photographs.

The first of my relatives to live in Eynsham was a great-great-aunt who came from Fairford, Gloucestershire in the 1880s. Her brother (my great-grandfather) soon moved here as well and today I still have relatives living in the village. Although, admittedly, I do not live in Eynsham I worked here from 1992 until recently and my love of the place continues to flourish. I am now very privileged to be Vice-Chairman of the Eynsham History Group at the relatively young age of 30.

It has been very exciting to go through Eynsham photographs with people and hear their own reminiscences. Complete strangers have been so kind and made me so welcome.

All profits that I make from this book will go to the British Diabetic Association so in buying this book I thank you for helping this charity.

It is intended that there will be a Volume 2, so if anyone has any further memories or photographs of Eynsham that they would like to be included, then please do contact me via any committee member of the Eynsham History Group.

Martin J Harris
November 1997

An aerial view of Eynsham in 1965.

Introduction

Eynsham has had many different spellings over the centuries and should be pronounced like its 19th century spelling 'Ensham' although the sham part is usually pronounced 'shum'. The word 'ham' means meadow but the meaning of the first part of the name is uncertain due its variation. The place of Egonesham was recorded in the Anglo-Saxon Chronicle in 571 although more information is known after the founding of Eynsham Abbey in 1005 by Ethelmar, Earl of Cornwall. An adjacent borough of Newland was established by the then abbot in 1215. After the Dissolution of the abbey in 1538/9, Eynsham gradually grew, based around the present-day Square. The building of the Toll Bridge in 1769 helped establish the village's importance and, until the building of the A40 this century, the main route for traffic travelling between London and South Wales went through Eynsham, hence the large number of pubs there have been. Today Eynsham continues to thrive with more houses built in 1997 and growing businesses with the industrial estates near the site of the old railway station. Also, thankfully, many of its old dwellings have survived, keeping the beauty and historical interest around for all to see.

Sources of Further Information

These items can be accessed in, amongst other places, Eynsham Library, Oxford Library, Oxfordshire Archives (the County Record Office) or the Bodleian Library.

The Eynsham Record, published annually since 1984 by Eynsham History Group and edited by Dr F Brian Atkins.

Good History, Vols. 1–4, published by Eynsham Junior History Group, 1995–1997.

From Acre End, Mollie Harris, Chatto and Windus, 1982.

Victoria County History of Oxford, Vol. XII, Oxford University Press, 1990.

Cartulary of the Abbey of Eynsham (1 and 2), H E Salter (Ed.).

Eynsham Abbey: 1005–1228, Eric Gordon, Phillimore, 1990.

Eynsham under the Monks, E Chambers, Oxfordshire Record Society, Vol.18, 1936.

Census Returns 1841–1891.

Directories of the 19th and 20th centuries (e.g. Kelly's).

Newspapers (on microfiche in the Centre For Oxfordshire Studies, Oxford Library), e.g. *Jackson's Oxford Journal, Oxford Mail, Oxford Times, Witney Gazette.*

The Square

The above photograph is believed to be the 1897 celebration of Queen Victoria's Diamond Jubilee. In the last 100 years much of the Square has changed very little. The large house at the back, built in the 1730s, now called Llandaff, did not have bay windows then or the ornate windows above the door and at the bottom right of the building. Up to at least the 1920s it was called Victoria House, although the area was

often referred to as Harper's Yard as the Harper family lived there then. In 1936 the house was acquired as a nursing home by the Burdens from Stanton Harcourt. Many babies were born there. Patriotism continued, as shown in the photograph on the right, with a crowd of people in the late 1930s/early 1940s.

Until 1988 the Square had a mediaeval Market Cross, shown here in a pre-World War I photograph. In 1991, the Cross was beyond repair, and Bill Brown, a Kidlington stonemason who had been evacuated to Eynsham during World War II, completed a carved replica made of Clipsham stone with the post-medieval top omitted.

Between the Red Lion pub and the church there was a cottage which has since been demolished. Church House, on the right of the church, was once a shoe repair shop run by the Calcutt family.

On 2 April 1921 the War Memorial next to the church was unveiled by James Francis Mason of nearby Eynsham Hall. Following a crowded church service conducted by Rev W Nash Bricknell, Mr Mason gave an address and then the Boy Scouts sounded the Last Post on their bugles.

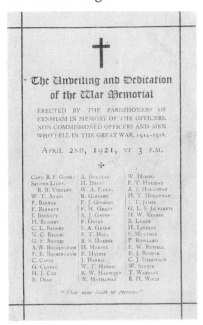 

The Bartholomew Room

The Batholomew Room was built in 1701/2 as a Charity School. It was named after John Bartholomew who, following his death in 1724, bequeathed £350 for the education of Eynsham boys. In the upper floor of the building is a board listing the 'benefactors to the school of Ensham'. Originally, the lower floor was just a pillar support until in later years the arches were filled in.

Over the years it has been a market hall, prison, fire station, Roman Catholic church and library. It is now used for exhibitions and by the Parish Council.

Acre End Street, High Street and Oxford Road

Acre End Street looking west from the Station Road. This view was taken after 1921 which was when Alfred Howe moved his Post Office and Chemist shop from next to Mansard House a little further along the road. Lloyd's Chemist is still on this site.

Acre End Street looking east showing the same Howe shop, although this part of the road was still known as High Street even in the 1950s. The Railway Inn and Swan Hotel are seen on the right. Further down the road on the right is a thatched cottage which was once the grocery store owned by T Hall & Sons.

The photograph on the right shows the Hall grocery store as it looked in the earlier part of the 20th century.

In the late 1930s, the Wrapson family moved into the cottage taking over the business from the widowed Peggy Hall who would later marry Ron Harris. Seen here in the back garden are Mr and Mrs Wrapson's young children Anne and John. Mansard House can be seen just behind the garage.

In 1953, the shop window was decorated for the Queen's coronation. As well as being grocers, Alfred (known as Tudor) and Rose Wrapson were also provision merchants, confectioners, and sold cakes to order as well as coal and coke.

Mansard House in Acre End Street, named after its unusual roof style where the lower part of the roof is steeper than the upper. [François Mansart (1598–1666) was a famous French architect.] The house has parts dating from the late 17th century. During the 19th century, the leasehold of the property was sold to members of the Morrell family of the Oxford brewery. Afterwards, in 1856, a chemist, Thomas Goodall, acquired the property. In the first part of the 20th century, it was lived in by the Howe family.

A view of Crown Crescent, on the right of this photograph, taken during the snowy weather in 1963. These brick terraced houses were, in the 19th century, owned by the adjacent Crown brewery. Charles Goodwin ran this business until G H Hanley and Co., an Oxford brewing firm, took over for a further decade until the 1890s.

Harold Quainton pictured here (above left) with his uncle Gilbert was born in Crown Crescent living at both No. 5 (the fifth house from the right of the row of terraced houses) and, in the 1930s, the house on the far right, which was previously lived in by Sam 'Buck' Buckingham, the fishmonger, and his family. The picture below shows Sam Buck and his son Jackie with his fish cart. Harold's father 'Ducky' (shown above right in his younger years) was a rope maker.

Acre End Street from the Mill Street end in 1978. [SC]

A view of High Street from the Square in the 1930s. Just behind the 2 cars is the Shrubbery, the doctor's surgery until 1978.

High Street looking west towards the Square.

High Street from Queen Street. Note the large house on the right, Hill House. Unlike today there is no gateway entrance from High Street. In the late 1920s or early 1930s the council moved the wall back to make more road room. As compensation, the owner of Hill House, Ernest Harris, received some money which was enough for him to buy a motorbike. Many used to hold conversations standing under the tree in front. The tall chimney behind is part of the now demolished brewery once owned by the Gibbons family.

Oxford Road from Queen Street, taken before 1935. The Cadbury van approaching Eynsham may be heading to Steven's grocers.

The Elms in Oxford Road is mainly a 16th century building. It was once part of an estate owned by Corpus Christi College.

Oxford Road from the bridge over the railway. The house between the 2nd and 3rd set of poles is Willowbank lived in by the widowed Mrs Smallhorn, from 1902 until her death in 1928.

Queen Street

Queen Street, perhaps named after the 18th century monarch Queen Anne, was formerly known as Pug/Puck(e) Lane, the name now given to the alleyway off High Street near the undertakers Green & Co. Many other roads now lead off Queen Street, including Queen's Lane (formerly Love Lane and also Pug Lane), Queen's Close, Tanners Lane, Orchard Close and Bitterell. Tanners Lane obtains its name from a tannery whose building survived until the 1970s. The Hythe Croft at the far end of the lane is a 17th century building with a 1907 extension designed by Clough William Ellis, the famous architect of Portmeirion in Wales who was also responsible for some of the houses in Cumnor.

Queen Street looking north. The first house on the left, Woodview, which was named due to a lovely view of woods that used to be seen, has been lived in by members of the Preston family since about 1920. Mona Gascoigne (née Preston) moved in to the house following her marriage in 1947. Her son, Roger, now lives there with an annexe for Mona at the rear of the house.

Queen Street looking south. The tree on the right has since been replaced by a row of semi-detached houses built by builder Harvey Hill.

Michael and June, children of Ernest 'Codgell' and Mildred Harris by the driveway of the Gardens in the 1930s. June has lived in Eynsham for most of her life. Michael now lives in Hailey.

Cobden House being re-thatched in 1997. The house was once lived in by Bishop Eric Gordon who wrote a history of Eynsham Abbey and was an active member of Eynsham History Group.

At the northern end of Queen Street is the Gables which is mainly a 17th century timber-framed house. It is said that William Cobbett (1763-1835) (a political personality who is remembered today for a book he wrote called *Rural Rides*) once stayed there when paper mill owner James Swann was living there and it is said that he planted an acacia tree which can be seen in the background. The malthouse shown on the left of the picture was built in around 1820 with a very unusual low-bevelled paper roof.

Major Edward Francis Oakeley (shown above) and his family moved to Eynsham in 1913 when they purchased the Gables for £4,000 from Major Gosset whose only son would be killed in World War I. The Major was a key figure in Eynsham for many years and the youngest of his four children, Mary, returned to live permanently in Eynsham after her retirement as a headmistress in the late 1970s.

Major Oakeley's brother was a hereditary peer, Sir Charles Oakeley. This baronage continued with the Major's eldest son (Edward) Atholl who was an expert wrestler, being the heavyweight wrestling champion of Europe 1932-33. The Major's great-grandfather, Sir Charles Oakeley, was created 1st Baronet (of Shrewsbury) in 1790 in honour of his services in India. Although the Major had retired from military service (he had served for the South Lancashire Regiment in South Africa 1899–1902), he continued to lead an active life, being a magistrate, churchwarden and district scout commissioner. His wife was also very active in Eynsham and was the person that many villagers would turn to when in need. The Major never learnt to drive a car, preferring to either cycle or be chauffeured in his own car by a Mr Riley until after the Great War when Henry Goodwin would take him around. The Oakeleys moved from the Gables after World War II to Tremaines, on the Woodstock Road out of Oxford. After the Major's death in 1954 Mrs Oakeley returned to Eynsham, living in Cherwell Lodge in Newland Street.

Newland Street

Newland Street from the west end. The cottages on the left were demolished in the 1960s.

In 1967 the cleared site revealed a building, to the left of the house under construction, known as the Pest House in which it is said that those with contagious diseases had to reside. Redthorne House, on the Mill Street/Newland Street corner, was once the home of the Swanns. Miss Gertrude Swann ran a private school there.

The house on the left, known as Newland Cottage, was lived in by relieving officer John Stanfield and his wife Janet. They were also responsible for registering the births and deaths for the Eynsham area. After his wife died, John married Miss Ethel Wastie who was the sub-postmistress at Church Hanborough. He died well into his 80s in the mid-1930s and Ethel lived in the Newland Street house until her death in 1953. Prior to the Stanfields, it has been said that Jack Gibbons, who owned the High Street brewery, lived there.

The gable-ended house next door was lived in by Clement Attlee's nephew (also an Attlee), his wife Peggy and family approximately during the late 1930s/early 1940s. The future Prime Minister would visit his relatives in Eynsham.

The row of cottages adjoining were numbered 1 to 6 in the early part of the 20th century. At that time, the Bettertons lived at No. 1, Mr Hedges at No. 2, and basket maker Mr Green at No. 3. Mr Harwood was at No. 4, Mrs Lay at No. 5, and the Evans family at No. 6.

Further down the road on the left-hand side were tall houses just beyond Messrs Sawyer's shop by the trees. They belonged to Mr Hirons, the butcher, who sold them to his neighbour at Newland House, Mr Ewan Cameron-Galton who had them demolished to provide more ground for trees and a shrubbery. Although specialising in pork, Mr Hirons also sold lard and faggots.

Temperance Hawtin in 1940 outside what is now 21 Newland Street. This house adjoined the Attlees' and Temperance used to work for them.

Temperance's son Ken taken around the same time with friends and family. Back row, left to right: Ronny Foster, Ken Hawtin. Front row: Betty Barnett, Michael –, Muriel Barnett.

The Newland Street/Queen Street corner showing Cobden.

A view slightly further down showing parts of the Gables on the left. The building on the opposite Newland Street/Queen Street corner was, until recently, a restaurant called O'Learys. It is now an Italian restaurant called Little Italy.

Chesneys

The house Chesneys was built in 1898 on the site of Newland Lodge which had burnt down. London art decorator Colonel Schmidt, who was probably responsible for the house's unique design both inside and out, lived there with his family. His initials are over the former front entrance. In the early part of the 20th century it appears that the family were greatly involved in village life until the First World War, when being Germans living in Britain was not easy. The family went on to change their name to Marshall. The following photographs, showing the interior and grounds, are believed to date from the late 19th century.

One of the fireplaces.

The two stone animals were later moved to the front entrance of the house. The identities of the children in the photograph below are unknown.

The same two children are shown by a gazebo which is presently located in the garden of the neighbouring Coach House.

It is not known whether the gentleman and lady are Mr and Mrs Schmidt or are friends or relatives.

A slightly later photograph showing a set of armour. It has been said that Newland Street blacksmith Mr Burden once dressed up in this armour for a fancy dress event. Unfortunately he could not get out of it and so the Combe blacksmith had to be called to his rescue.

Mill Street

Views of Mill Street from the southern end

Fred Harris' butcher's shop (now the estate agents Chancellors). The window above the shop sign was an early horizontal sliding sash window.

A similar view just slightly further up. Unlike today, very few vehicles are parked in the road.

Mill Street from the Malster and Shovel. The first white house on the right is an early 18th century building called the White House and has fluted pilasters. Further up is Myrtle House with a Georgian front. This was once the home of Dame Helen Gardiner, an eminent literary scholar.

The Vicarage

The Vicarage taken in the early 1900s. This Queen Anne style house was sold in 1985 and has since been used as offices by BUPA and Bryant Country Homes. Part of the rear of the vicarage garden is now the site of Eynsham Medical Centre.

Cottages in Mill Street

The right-hand side of the white cottage (shown here in 1963) was removed to make room for a set of shops which includes the present day Post Office.

Mill Street from the Catholic Apostolic church. Next to it is the Holt with a most ornate Victorian frontage, designed by William Wilkinson (architect of Oxford's Randolph

Hotel), equipped with balcony and marble columns adorning the windows. The Hayward family were living there in 1940 when Diana Hayward married Rowland Oakeley. Diana's father was a medical doctor who moved to Eynsham after retiring from Wimbledon.

Mill Street covered in snow in the early 1980s. Sarah Brown and Karen Baker are seen on the right of the photograph pulling a sledge watched by Sarah's mother Janet by the Holt. [SC]

The architecturally unappreciated water tower that stood until 1972 where flats now stand stored water from Eynsham's own local well along the Cassington Road. The adjoining Sunny Side flats were opened 3 November 1964 by Counsellor H J Wood.

Other Streets

Abbey Street

Abbey Street was the main road to Stanton Harcourt until, in the days of the Abbey, Abbot Adam had it blocked off and replaced it with what is now Station Road.

Abbey Street looking south.

Station Road

Views of Station Road both with and without the house on the right. The road was so called because it led to the railway station.

Witney Road

The Coronation Crescent part of Witney Road is shown not long after it was built in 1937 by Eynsham builder Harvey Hill.

A procession in Witney photographed by Stanley Green from the family home in Witney Road. The houses in what is now Old Witney Road can just be seen in the background.

Church Street

This view of this street has hardly changed during the 20th century.

Lombard Street

Previously part of Mill Street then Abbey Street. Baker's restaurant was once a grocer, beer wines and spirits business run by the Gibbons family. Since then it has been a pub called the Board and a restaurant which a few years ago was run by the famous actor Kenneth Cope.

Back Lane

Clover Place

A house in Clover Place in 1974. The thatch on the roof has since been replaced with tiles.

The Toll Bridge and Rivers

The Toll Bridge

Although often called the Eynsham toll bridge it is really the Swinford toll bridge. Having cost £4,850 to build, it was opened in 1769. Previously, a ferry service had been in operation by which even John Wesley had crossed. Back then, larger vehicles would travel between Witney and Oxford via Long Hanborough, Bladon, Campsfield and Begbroke. Formerly the A4141, the bridge now carries the B4044 and is the Eynsham/Cumnor parish boundary and prior to 1974 was the Oxfordshire/Berkshire county divide. Built for the 4th Earl of Abingdon, the bridge with its nine arches was, until the A40 was built in the mid-1930s, the main route for those vehicles travelling between London and Gloucester/South Wales.

James Lord, an Eynsham mason, whose descendants are the Wastie family who run the local garage (James Lord's daughter Mary married a William Wastie at Eynsham in 1772), was probably involved in the building of the bridge as an estimate prepared by the man survives to this day.

Controversy has continued with the bridge over the last few decades. Following decimalisation, its 2p charge for standard cars continued until the owners were legally given permission to increase it to 5p. Unlike in the 1970s, receipts are now no longer issued and the toll collectors are protected by a small shelter in the middle of the road. All income is still tax free!

Mr John Floyd, one of the many toll collectors over the years, outside the toll house in the late 19th century. For many years various members of the Floyd family have lived at the cottages at Swinford.

The following photographs show some of the pictures taken over the years of the road over the toll bridge.

Jim Evans (second from the left) standing with three other people on the frozen Thames by the bridge in 1963.

The gentleman shown here by the bridge, taken before 1905, was Richard Treadwell Snr, the river and Eynsham weir keeper (referred to by the Oxford photographer Henry Taunt in his writings). He in turn was followed by his son, Richard Jnr, whose sisters Hannah, Lizzie and Nellie collected the tolls at this bridge for some years.

The pictures below show views of Pinkhill lock with its wooden framed house.

Eynsham weir.

Chilbridge which is said to be medieval.

Until the building of the A40, Mill Street used to lead directly to an Abbey mill which was situated on the Evenlode, a tributary of the Thames. The mill was a corn mill until 1682 and then a paper mill manufacturing paper for Oxford Bibles, until 1893 when it became a glue factory. In recent years it has been a fish farm.

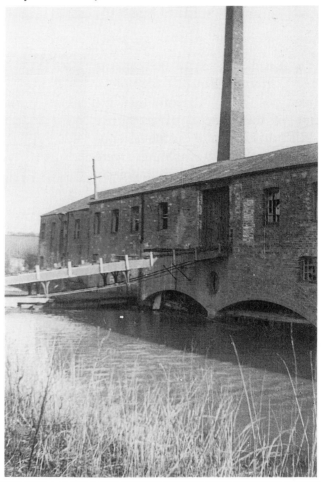

Churches

The Abbey

Eynsham Abbey, a Benedictine order (a monastic movement originating from St Benedict of Nursia, Italy), was founded in 1005 AD on the site approximately south of the present parish church. Following Henry VIII's dissolution of the monasteries in the 16th century, the abbey buildings were demolished over a period of time although fragments still exist, including those that were incorporated into later Eynsham houses. A beautiful arch, possibly from the door of the old Abbey, which used to be in the vicarage garden (as shown on the right) is now positioned inside St Leonard's church above the entrance.

St Leonard's Church

The Parish Church which stands in the Square mostly dates from the 13th to the 15th century. St Leonard is the patron saint of prisoners and was a favourite of the Benedictines.

The South Aisle, whose exterior is seen from the churchyard is believed to be the oldest section of the church, being part of an early chapel.

The early 20th century views of the church's interior show the John Wilkins designed east window built in 1903 by Lavers and Westlake in memory of Dr Smallhorn who was the village doctor for 37 years until his death in 1902.

Left to right: Stuart Blanch, Bishop Eric Gordon and Robert Key in 1988 at a service to commemorate the restoration of the church. [SC]

Eynsham has had many notable vicars, including the controversial William Simcox Bricknell (vicar 1845–1888) and his grandson William Nash Bricknell (1893–1928) who is remembered on a window in the Chancel. Stuart Yarworth Blanch was Eynsham vicar from 1951 to 1956. He went on to be Bishop of Liverpool and then Archbishop of York. He died in 1994. Robert Frederick Key was vicar from 1985 to 1991 when Ian Bentley came.

Pamela Richards and the late Mrs Chalmers are generally credited with introducing colourful kneelers into the church. Each kneeler's subject is based on something Eynsham-related. In 1997 Gladys Garner produced one in memory of author and broadcaster Mollie Harris. The snakeshead fritillary represent Mollie's love of the countryside and of the fritillary that grow in the village fields of Ducklington where she was born and grew up.

The Roman Catholic Church (St Peter's)

In the last 100 years Eynsham Roman Catholics have worshipped at various places including Newland Lodge in Newland Street until it burnt down in about 1897 (rebuilt as Chesneys), the Railway Inn in Acre End Street and the Bartholomew Room. Building of the present church of St Peter was started in 1939 and by 1943 it was in use with a temporary wooden nave. The Gilbert Flavel designed building was finally completed in 1967 with a new room added on in 1994. Father John Lopes who was the parish priest from 1928 until his death in 1961 was also a Parish Councillor. He lived at the house Llandaff in the Square and afterwards The White House in Mill Street. A road off Mill Street was later named after him. The author J R R Tolkien's son John was the priest at St Peter's before Father David Mead.

The Baptist Church

The Baptist Chapel in Lombard Street was built in 1815. The Alden family, the Oxford butchers, were strong supporters of this church and used to send meat to the Eynsham poor.

The Wesleyan Chapel

The Wesleyan Chapel was built of brick and stone for the Methodists in 1884 in Thames Street. In 1979 it was sold to the Parochial Church Council for its present use as a church hall.

The Catholic Apostolic Church

This was built in the mid-1800s in Mill Street. It has a delightful baptistry topped by a turret with a conical roof. Those who attended this church, including members of the Pimm family (although they continued to attend St Leonard's as well), belonged to a religious movement that, in preparation for Jesus' second coming, had 12 founding apostles as well as bishop-like 'angels'. The final Apostle died in 1901 and the last angel died in 1945. Angels that lived in Eynsham included James Hinton (in the mid-19th century) and James Clough came to live in Newland Street until his death in 1906. Its use ceased following the death in the early 1980s of its last deacon Bevan Pimm. The building was then purchased by the parish council until its recent purchase and conversion into a private dwelling. [SC]

To claim your Great Day Out simply present this voucher at the Heritage Attraction of your choice. At The Oxford Story Exhibition, The White Cliffs Experience, A Day at the Wells and The Canterbury Tales one child or adult will be admitted free with every full paying adult. At the Jorvik Viking Centre your voucher will entitle you to 10% off the price of admission for one adult.

This offer is valid until 31 March 1999 (excluding 18-21 February at the Jorvik Viking Centre, York). A child relates to persons under 15. Pre-booked tickets are not available with this promotion. One offer per person. Photocopies will not be accepted. This is not valid for use with any other promotions or in conjunction with a family ticket. Damaged/defaced vouchers will not be accepted. No cash alternative.

Heritage

MARKETING
LEADING VISITOR ATTRACTIONS

GREAT DAYS OUT WITH HERITAGE LEADING ATTRACTIONS.

Forget the winter blues with this great offer that will offer that will give you and your family a fun day out and save you money too!

We teamed up with the Heritage Attractions Group to give you a great deal on admission to some of the UK's leading visitor attractions where you'll experience a warm welcome and a very special brand of entertainment.

Conveniently located in some of Britain's most historic towns and cities, the centres provide an intriguing and amusing insight into the past and are designed to appeal to both children and adults. Each has its own character and theme created through a combination of technological innovation and historical authenticity. But they all share the highest levels of award winning presentation that make them the most popular attractions of their kind enjoyed by over 1 million people every year.

Journey back in time at one of the UK's leading heritage attractions. Located in some of Britain's most historic towns these fascinating attractions offer a unique experience for all your family and your senses. Choose the sights and smells of Viking-age York, the medieval days of Chaucers Canterbury, the scandal of Georgian society in Tunbridge Wells, Dover's dramatic frontline history or unique journey through 800 years of Oxford University's history.

- **CANTERBURY TALES** TAKES AN ENTERTAINING LOOK AT CHAUCER'S MEDIEVAL ENGLAND.
  St. Margaret's Street, Canterbury, Kent. CT1 2TG. Tel: 01227 479227

- THE **OXFORD STORY** EXHIBITION VIVIDLY TELLS THE STORY OF OXFORD UNIVERSITY'S FORMIDABLE PAST.
  6 Broad Street, Oxford. OX1 3AJ. Tel: 01865 790055.

- THE **JORVIK** VIKING CENTRE RE-CREATES THE ATMOSPHERE, SOUNDS AND SMELLS OF THE VIKING CITY OF JORVIK.
  Coppergate, York YO1 9WT. Information Hotline: 01904 643211

- A DAY AT THE **WELLS** PRESENTS THE SCANDAL, GLITTERING COSTUMES AND SOCIAL INTRIGUE OF THE COLOURFUL GEORGIAN ERA.
  The Corn Exchange, The Pantiles, Royal Tunbridge Wells, Kent. TN2 5QJ. Tel 01892 546545.

- THE **WHITE CLIFFS** EXPERIENCE IS A VIVID SPECTACLE OF BRITAIN'S DRAMATIC FRONTLINE HISTORY, FROM THE ROMAN INVASION TO THE DRAMATIC MOMENTS OF WORLD WAR II.
  Market Square, Dover. CT16 1PB. Tel: 01304 210101. Fax: 01304 212267

Sports

Football Club

This photograph, taken in 1920, is of the Eynsham Crusaders Under 15 team. Included are, back row, left to right: Mr Duckett, Harry Brooks, Bill Sawyer, George Dixey, Ben Tovey, Harold Dixey, George Green. Middle row: Chris Biggers, Fred Ayres, Gilbert Hall. Front row: Andy Duckett, Cyril Whitlock, H Larner, Phil Pimm, Jack England.

Eynsham's 1932–33 football team. Back row, left to right: Jack Green, – Maskell, – Batts, H Dixey, Charles Pimm, B Harling, J Welsted, Albert Axtell. Front row: Billy Betterton, Philip Pimm, Leonard Pimm, Harry Merry, Alan Pratley, Vernon Green, Frank 'Jammy' James, J Murdock.

Eynsham Football Club celebrated its centenary in 1997 as this carnival float in the car park just outside the medical centre shows. Gary Bailey is holding the cup and pointing.

Cricket

Eynsham cricket team probably taken in the early 1920s. Back row, left to right: Mr Manning, Georgie Mayne, Albert Axtell, Vernon Green, Jack Green, George Pimm, Leonard Pimm, Richard Wood. Middle row: George Green, Bert Lambourne, Wilfred Watkins, Fred Ayres, – Taylor. Front row: Charlie Pimm, John Biggers. This was taken at the old cricket pavillion down Station Road. Richard Wood, a painter at the building firm Hutchins & Green, was the umpire and his daughter Hilda, who married Ted Sumner, often used to take the scores at the matches.

Hockey

The Eynsham ladies hockey team from the early 1930s. Back row, left to right: Peggy Hall, Mrs Blake, Eva Rowland, Ruth Hale, Ivy Perrin, Mrs Quainton, Hilda Stevens, Joyce Titchell, Queenie Buckingham, Clara Harris. Middle row: Iris(?) Woods, Elsie Rhodes (married widower Mr Howe), Polly England, — Betteridge, — Woods. Bottom row: Freda Douglas, Eva Woods (married Brandy Green). All were Eynsham people except Ruth Hale from Cassington.

Netball

Some of the members of the Eynsham Netball Club in 1981. Left to right: Janet Brown, Pam Bunce, Julie Horwood, Sue Johnson, Ann Phillips (later Cross), Denise Dutton, Cheryl Marlow. [SC]

Other Societies and Clubs

The Eynsham Morris

The Eynsham Morris is the term given to the morris dancers who have probably been part of the village life since the 18th century. The group remained active into the 20th century until the time of World War II. Thanks to Keith Green, the Eynsham Morris was re-started in 1979 and continues to be an important part of Eynsham's culture.

The Eynsham Morris for King George VI's coronation in 1937. Left to right: Buff Russell, Phil Lambourne, Arthur Lambourne, Ern Edwards, Jack Drewitt, Bert Russell, Cyril Russell, Pearce Lambourne, Sid Russell.

Old and new members pictured together in 1980. Back row, left to right: Dave Townsend, Stan Launchbury, Robin Saunders, Derek Malin, Mike Simpson, Robin Mitchell, Bob King, Dennis Green, Keith Green, Ken Sheffield. Front row: Ian Green, Phil Lambourne, Ernest May, Bert Russell, Duncan Briggs. [SC]

A musical band of the 19th century.

Members of the Hospital Sunday band of the early 20th century. In late July/early August, the band would go round Eynsham playing tunes to raise money for the Radcliffe Infirmary. Their cheerful music hall tunes were not always popular with the vicar, the Revd Bricknell. Included on this picture, taken at Hythe Croft in Tanners Lane, are Thomas Hanks (second gentleman on the right) standing in front of his eldest son who is next to the other child Billy Betterton.

Various members of the Christian Women's Tuesday Fellowship in the Square, Autumn 1979. Left to right: 1 Gwen Spanner, 2 –, 3 Alice Winterbourne, 4 Sally Ridley (the then vicar's wife), 5 Gwen Whitlock, 6 Elsie Brinkler, 7 Lillian Pimm, 8 Vi Warren, 9 Ethel Ayres, 10 Alice Batts, 11 Ida Hopkins, 12 Margaret Woolley, 13 Edith Brooks, 14 Josie Cox, 15 Alice Parker, 16 Iris James, 17 Mrs Russell, 18 Emily Corbett, 19 Mary Miles, 20 Rose Brinkler, 21 –, 22 Elsie Evans, 23 –, 24 Gladys Garner, 25 Nellie Coppins, 26 Ida Elford. [SC]

Eynsham's bellringers in the 1950s. Back row, left to right: Bert Harris, Bert Hicks, Phillis Hale, Cliff Bennett, Bert Miles. Front row: Cyril Hale, John Miles, David Floyd. Phillis (who married Andy Pimm) continues to be an active bellringer for St Leonard's.

Eynsham's Royal British Legion Women's Section celebrating its 40th anniversary in 1988. Lillian Pimm is holding the large card with Helen Russell to the right. [SC]

Eynsham History Group

The Eynsham History Group was founded in 1959 and has continued to go from strength to strength. Its first chairman was Mr Hugh Cooper, an architect who lived at Murray House in Acre End Street. As well as its fortnightly meetings from September through to March and organised outings to places of interest, one of its key successes has been the annual publication of the *Eynsham Record.* This journal of the Eynsham History Group, first published in 1984, is edited by Dr Brian Atkins and is sold throughout Eynsham due to the organisation of Pamela Richards, the publications manager.

Committee members past and present, taken at the Eynsham History Group's 1996 party held at the Primary School. Back row, left to right: Cate Foster, Shirley White, Josie Smith, Donald Richards, Brian Atkins, Stanley Green, Ted Whelan, Michael Farthing, Martin J Harris, Pamela Richards. Front row: Lilian Wright, Edna Mason, Phillis Pimm, Mary Oakeley, Beryl Hastings.

Public Houses

Believed to be Eynsham's oldest pub the Red Lion in the Square dates from the 16th century when it was called the Angel. As well as being a drinking house the Red Lion has functioned as a place for administering parish affairs, and enjoying whist drives and morris dancing.

The Preston family ran the Red Lion for many years at the turn of the last century. Left to right: William senior with his children Harry, George, William junior and wife Emma. Back then it was more like a hotel and Emma had a pony and trap which she used to pick up residents from Oxford railway station.

Pictured here outside the Red Lion in 1980 for a presentation following a fundraising event are the Eynsham Morris with whist drive organiser Mildred Harris, long serving landlord Frank Harris (no relation), and a gentleman receiving a donation on behalf of a blind charity by Frank's wife Dorothea, known as Auntie, who is standing next to her daughter Wendy followed by Tricia Saunders. [SC]

The Swan, in Acre End Street, was once an old coaching inn. The Railway Inn, next door and, unlike its neighbour, now closed, is believed to be previously called the Britannia which was built by the Eynsham brewer James Gibbons in the mid 19th century.

Some of the members of the Swan Darts Club along with their trophies. Left to right: — Axtell, Michael Hooper, Harold Quainton, Elsie Green (née Jefferies), Harvey Hill, —, —.

The Newland Inn (now Newlands) in Newland Street which until the 1860s was two cottages. In the late 19th and early 20th century the landlord was Thomas Hanks, the grandfather of long-term Eynsham resident Temperance Hawtin.

The White Hart in Newland Street, formerly the Haunch of Venison, was the original courthouse of Newland when it was a separate borough from Eynsham.

The Star in Witney Road dates from the 1860s and is now famous for being the starting point of the annual pram race held on carnival day.

The Talbot, formerly the Horse and Jockey, near the Toll Bridge once had as its landlord Johnny Juggins, a well known Eynsham character who lived until he was 90. He was buried in Eynsham in 1948.

The Malster and Shovel (originally the Malt Shovel) at the corner of Thames Street and Mill Street was recorded as early as the 18th century although in the 20th century was converted to a private house.

Shops and Trades

A harness produced by A Hughes in 1841.

HOWE'S FAMILY APERIENT LIVER PILLS

Will be found a most efficacious remedy in all Bilious and Liver Complaints. They may be taken at any time or season, without the slightest alteration of diet, or extra care from cold, which are so necessary in most other medicines.—*Sold only in Boxes at 7½d., 1/1½, and 2/9.*

HOWE'S TOOTHACHE AND TIC PILLS,

For Neuralgia, Toothache, etc., scarcely ever fail to give instant relief, and effect a complete cure.
In Boxes, 1/1½ and 2/9.

THE EYNSHAM BOUQUET. A REFRESHING AND LASTING PERFUME.

In Bottles, 1|-, 1/6, 2/-, etc.

THE EYNSHAM SAUCE.

Unrivalled for imparting an exquisite relish to Chops, Steaks, Gravies, Cold Meats, etc.—*Bottles, 6d. and 1|-.*

The above are prepared and sold by

HENRY A. HOWE,

Family & Dispensing Chemist (by Exam.), EYNSHAM.

Left, a 1903 advertisement for Henry Albert Howe's chemist and stationery shop which was also the post office (below). His son, Alfred William Howe, succeeded his father.

Ron Gardner's Electrical Sales and Services shop in Acre End Street with his fleet of cars. His son now runs Algar (Electric Motors) Ltd just off the Stanton Harcourt Road.

One of the modern day industrial estates on the western side of the Stanton Harcourt Road. Amongst the businesses included on the Oasis Business Park are Usborne Books and W S Atkins.

Sawyer's shop, known for selling almost everything, was established in 1846 by E Sawyer, great-great-grand-father of Jean Buttrick who still lives in Eynsham. To its left was Burden's the blacksmith, a family business for several generations.

Bill Sawyer was born in Eynsham in 1905 and took over the well-established Newland Street shop in 1939 and kept it going with help from his family until it closed in the early 1970s. He spent the last few years before his death in 1989 at Beech Court Nursing Home just a, few yards from the site of the shop.

Foster Dawe, standing in front of the vehicle, was orphaned when 12 and brought up by the Stevens family who ran a grocers and bakery. The shop entrance was in High Street on the left side of the present Co-op shop.

George Green, shown above, also worked for the business.

A 1936 car advertisement for Blake's which was in Mill Street.

Reg Bloyce (see below).

The sugar beet factory was established in the late 1920s on the site of the present day Oxford Magnet Technology factory next to the Talbot. Reg Bloyce came to Eynsham as an engineer from Colchester to work there, lodging with the Stayt family in Queen Street. Following the factory's sudden demise, he obtained employment with Co-op Insurance and married Clara Harris at Eynsham in 1932. Reg died in 1997 after over 65 years of marriage.

The Seeney family had a garage (above) in a yard off Thames Street until the 1980s. A smokehole (right) was rescued by Sue Chapman during its demolition and is now held in the museum store at Standlake. [SC]

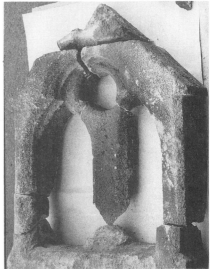

Below: E L Faulkner's garage in High Street in 1963 which had previously been Henry Goodwin's garage. The frosted tree was a delight for children as Henry often used to pick apples from it to give to the children passing by. The area is now Blenheim Drive with houses built in the mid-1990s.

Schools and Children

At the beginning of the 20th century the state schools in Eynsham were the National Infants' School in Station Road, which was first used in 1846–7, and the Board School in Witney Road for those up to school-leaving age, built in 1877. In 1958, Batholomew School by the Board School in Witney Road was opened, followed by the closure of the Station Road school. The Eynsham County Primary School off Beech Road, having been built in 1967 was destroyed by fire in 1969 and then rebuilt by Easter 1970.

The Old School House in Station Road. After retiring as rector of Lincoln College, Oxford, Sir Walter Oakeshott lived there until his death in 1987. A former Vice-Chancellor of Oxford, he was internationally respected as an expert on medieval art and books.

An Eynsham school picture from probably just before World War I. Back row, left to right: —, Elsie Jeffreys, —, —, —, Violet Ayres, —, —, Ada Harwood, —, —, —, Rosie Grant. Middle row: Gertie Harris, —, —, Rose Leach, Ida Bryant, Victoria Moulder, Ida Watkins, Gladys Brooks, —, Gladys Floyd, Alice Betterton, Lizzie Leach, May Skinner. Front row: Gladys Russell, Evelyn Biggers, Ella Treadwell, —, Freda Bennett, Ida Buckingham, Daisy Ayres, Nora Floyd, —.

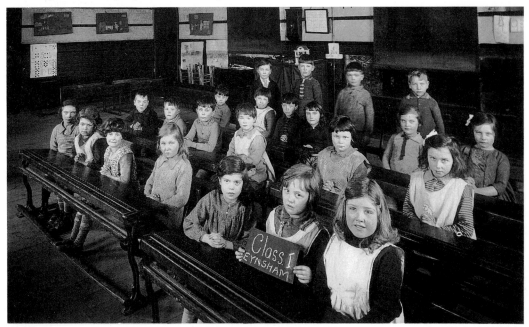

An infants class in 1929. Back row (standing), left to right: Chris Bryant(?), Ernest Ayris, Leonard Evans, Raymond Floyd. Third row: Cyril Barker(?), Beatrice State, Leslie Dance, Dora Ashton, Gladys Ainsley, Freda Harris. Second row: Jimmy Hedges, —, Jack Hardwick, Evelyn Ayres, Helen Russell, Gladys Evans. Front row: Eileen Butler, Connie Lay, Hebie Treadwell, Joan Drewitt, Josie Pimm, Maorie Axtell, Mabel Hedges.

A class from the senior school in 1939. Back row, left to right: John Nash, Maurice Howes, Gilbert Parker, Albert Jeffrey, Eric Prowton, Kenneth Long, Edmund 'Eddie' Evans, Georgie Styles, Don Edwards, Boycot 'Tricky' Evans, Leslie 'Snowy' Ayres. Middle row: Aubrey Howard, Roy Nash, Dennis Russell, Freddie Meakins, Eileen Harper, Brenda Merry, Brenda Lewington, Raymond Green, Bob Betterton, Basil Whelan, Douglas 'Duggie' Russell. Front row: Joyce Dore, Dorsey Pinker, Sonia 'Sonie' Harwood, Gwen Pratley, Barbara Hill, Zena Evans, Joan Pimm, Joan Winterbourne, Doreen Bryant, Elsie Bantin, June Harris.

A class of the late 1940s. Back row, left to right: Fred Prowton, Geoff Batts, Bill Harris, Gordon Russell, Colin Merry, Michael Weller, Merlin Thomas, George Roberts, Frank BroadHurst, Bob Pratley, Arthur Howard, Arthur Hall. Middle row: Ken Brown, George Bennett, Beryl Hedges, Judy Quainton, Greta Phipps, Yvonne Biggers, Gwenda Ackling, Sylvia Hale, Doreen Grant, Yvonne Broadhurst, –, John Burke. Front row: Sheila Tibbetts, Jean Porter, Ann Harwood, Rita Harwood, Maureen Morgan, Ann Gallagher, Dulcie Hunt.

The head teacher of the Beech Road primary school, Mr George R Baines, and his wife Judith (also a teacher) celebrating their retirement in July 1983 with a crowd of pupils. [SC]

Acre End Playgroup children during harvest festival time. Left to right: Patricia Saunders, Polly Bannister, Laura Carr, Diggy Hodges and Tom Lloyd. [SC]

A children's pancake race in 1979. The three boys holding the pans are (left to right) James Wotherspoon, Alex Holmes and Russell Phipps.

The Railway and Other Transport

The Railway

The railway through Eynsham arose from local business men wanting a branch line to join Witney up to the railway network at the Yarnton junction. In 1859, people such as the Witney Blanket Company's head, Charles Early, and Eynsham's Druce family formed a committee to achieve this. Following a Parliament Bill being passed and the purchase of land (in Eynsham from landowners the Duke of Marlborough, a Rev Bourne from Wiltshire and the Druces), the railway was built at a reported cost of about £40,000. The first official train went from Witney stopping at Eynsham on its way to Oxford on 14 November 1861. Initially, trains would leave Eynsham for Oxford four times a day at a cost of 10d for third class up to 1s 8d for first class. Many of the Eynsham working class would still continue to travel very little outside the village or would use the local carrier well into the 20th century.

1861 - November 18th   The Railway arrives at Eynsham

Peggy Garland in 1977 with a mural commemorating the 1861 opening of the railway. [SC]

As a result of the railway cutbacks of the early 1960s, the Eynsham railway carried its last passengers in 1962. Both Jim Evans and railway enthusiast William Beauchamp travelled on that last train and the Philcox family were also there to witness that event. The photographs here are of that last journey.

In the 1970s, the railway tracks around Eynsham were dismantled. Above is shown the road bridge over the railway which took the Oxford Road from Eynsham towards the toll bridge.

The timber-built station building was first erected for the station's opening in 1861 and extended in 1878/9. It was demolished in the late 1980s. [SC]

Road transport

Workers in the late 1920s laying pipes on the road, possibly for the sugar beet factory.

Before the advent of motorised transport, the carrier would transport goods and sometimes people between villages and towns. Both the wealthy and working class would have much of their out-of-village shopping carried out by this tradesman. From the mid-1890s until 1935, the Harris family were involved in the carrying business at Eynsham. Above is shown Ernest Harris senior's carrier's van, from a Henry Taunt photograph (a leading Oxford photographer) taken in 1906 in the Square in Eynsham when the Harris family lived in the house that is now Llandaff. [Oxfordshire Photographic Archive]

From 1917, the Witney carrier Edward Oliffe and his son Les assisted Ernest's daughter Gertie with Eynsham trade. Seen here are the Oliffes with their motorised Napier van on the corner of High Street and Queen Street.

Until the road improvement of converting part of the old railway track off the Stanton Harcourt road to link up with the Oxford road towards the toll bridge, many lorries from the Standlake quarries still travelled along Station Road and through Eynsham as this early 1980s photograph shows. [SC]

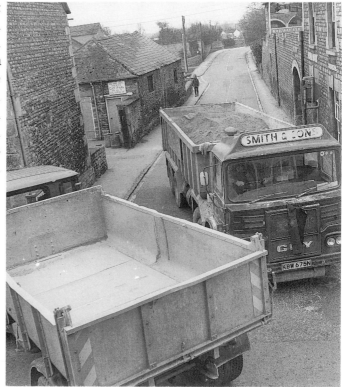

In 1997, public transport is carried out by Eynham's SP Coaches/Steve's Travel and the Thames Transit bus company, recently taken over by the Stagecoach company. Following much competition in 1995 between Thames Transit and the Oxford Bus Company, it was decided that the latter would withdraw its service through Eynsham.

Personalities and Celebrities

A collection of Eynsham photographs would be incomplete without mentioning the important contribution made by Jim Evans (1897–1987) who had great enthusiasm for photography and local history in Eynsham. After growing up in Eynsham, he married Gladys Floyd at Cumnor and lived at Swinford Cottages until his latter years when he lived a few doors away from Mollie Harris and the Chapmans in Mill Street.

One of his earlier jobs was as a chauffeur for a prince from the Indian state of Khairpur who at the time resided at Stroud Court in Farmoor. Long time Eynsham resident Elsie Floyd and her mother also worked at the house. Jim was a keen drummer all of his life and children would love to entertained by him.

Dr Derrick Bolsover MBE, an extremely popular doctor with patients and staff, moved into the Shrubbery, High Street in Eynsham in 1952 following the death of Dr Tighe. He retired in 1985 and died in 1987 aged 67. He was considered to be an extremely talented and out-standing GP and a man of great wit. Tributes were paid to him at a special thanks-giving service held in January 1988 at St Leonard's Church, Eynsham. The address was given by the then senior partner, Dr John Simpson. [SC]

There are now seven doctors making up the partnership that serves the Eynsham and Long Hanborough residents and people in the surrounding area. They are, back row, left to right: Neil Rust, Paul Coffey, Ian Binnian, Philip Stephenson, Max Peterson. Front row: Helen Evans, Jean Bailey.

Temperance Hawtin

Mrs Temperance Hawtin who celebrated her 93rd birthday in 1997 was born Temperance Beatrice Hanks on 8 July 1904 in Eynsham. As a child she lived in a house with her parents and brothers and sisters in High Street between the Square and Mill Street which was owned by the Biggers family. Her father was a hurdle maker. Her brothers were Rodney William, Walter Thomas, Reginald Percy and her sisters Ida Elizabeth and Elsie Violet and Daisy Florence the full names which Temperance has remembered all of her life. Her grampy Hanks at one time ran the Newland Inn in Newland Street.

The Hanks family supported the Wesleyan Methodist chapel rather than St Leonard's and were regular attenders. Whilst still at school Temperance did housework for Mrs Preston who lived on the Abbey Street/Swan Street corner. The Preston family had also occupied the Red Lion.

Other houses that Temperance has lived in include one of the tall set-back houses in Acre End Street (known as Wytham Terrace), the house in Mill Street that Mollie Harris lived in before her death and the house that is now 21 Newland Street (which was no. 6 then and owned by a Mr Harwood). The rent for the Newland Street house at one time was 3s 6d. After her marriage to Urbin Hawtin in the Wesleyan chapel (they had first met on the night of Cassington Feast) they had one son, Ken, who was born in the Acre End Street house where Temperance's mother was also living at the time. When Ken was only 11 years old Urbin died from meningitis. He was buried in Eynsham churchyard.

Temperance did various cleaning, looking after children and odd jobs just to make ends meet. When Ken was at school she spent a few hours a week for 7 years at Beauchamps' grocers shop. Next door to the Hawtins in Newland Street was Clement Attlee's nephew Captain Attlee who Temperance used to also clean for. This work was made difficult for her when she also had to do war work down at the NAAFI by the Talbot cooking for various military establishments. During all these hard times the Hawtins kept cheerful and were regulars at carnivals and Eynsham events for many years (Temperance, son Ken and daughter-in-law Peggy also attended the 1997 carnival) and they often won prizes. One year it was a toss up for the judges whether Temperance or her mother should win best prize for decorated house front. She also enjoyed decorating prams with flowers. For the King George VI coronation celebration on 12 May 1937 the best couple prize was awarded to Urbin and Temperance.

In the 1950s, Temperance moved to a recently built council bungalow in Greens Road. She worked for Dr Bolsover from the 1950s until her retirement in the mid-1970s and was well loved by all the Bolsover family. Temperance was also a very dear friend of Mollie Harris and attended her funeral in 1995. Temperance, much to her amusement, was even photographed by Sue Chapman for Mollie's book on privies wearing a raincoat and carrying a newspaper towards the outside toilet.

Jack Green

In 1997, Morrells brewery, in recognition of Jack Green's 95th birthday, allowed him to have a free pint a day at Eynsham's Red Lion pub.

Jack was born Bernard John Henry Green on 18 May 1902 in Colombia Terrace in one of the houses set back from the road in High Street just opposite where the Greens' family undertaking business is today.

The Green family were great church attenders and Jack's grandfather, father and uncle were all churchwardens. The pulpit was restored in 1987 in memory of Bernard George Green, churchwarden for 33 years, and his father, Henry, before him, churchwarden for 21 years.

Bill Allsworth, shown here with a lengthy beard, has for many years been the 'starter upper' on Eynsham Carnival Day, starting the pram race. Some children have referred to him as the balloon man as he would go round the streets with balloons. [SC]

Frankie Wastie, one of the many Eynsham Wasties, was born in Mill Street and was one of the Eynsham men who served in the Korean War. He now runs a nursery in Sutton.

Mr Frederick Ayres is shown here on the left with his Buffalo sash. On the right is his wife Bessie. The Ayres had nine children: Lilian, Will, Lou, Ernest ('Smag'), Win, Hilda, Fred, Vi and John. The family lived in Queen Street until they moved in the 1940s to a house on the Hanborough Road which daughter Vi continued to occupy after her marriage to Bob Warren at Eynsham Baptist Church in 1942.

Nellie Jefferies (later Mott) shown here in Hill House garden in Queen Street where she worked in the early 1930s. Notice the upside down jam jars by her feet used as a garden border.

Harvey Hill, here in his World War I uniform, built many houses in Eynsham along with his brother Cyril. Previously, he had served a carpentry apprenticeship at the Oxford firm Woolridge and Simpson Ltd. Back then, he would cycle from Eynsham to work.

Hilda Brooks in 1996 with son Donald, the year she celebrated her 99th birthday. She first came to live in Eynsham when she was 13.

Donald, also an Eynsham resident, established a plumbing business in 1968.

Charles Faulks (left) and James Davey with a cigar (right) in 1892.

For many years Faulks was Eynsham's most esteemed railway stationmaster. Davey was a well-known Eynsham saddler and harness maker in the late 19th and early 20th century. He was said to be the inventor of 'Davey's Registered Harness Buckle'. He was also a writer and reciter of popular monologues. His company was said to be much in demand because of his wit and wonderful personality. The following lines are extracts from his *Reminiscences of Eynsham*:

Looking westward o'er the meadows,
From the ancient Beacon Hill,
Where the willows cast long shadows,
On each silent pool or mill.
Where the river flows serenely,
Past the farm by Eynsham Bridge,
Like a vassal paying homage,
To the oak-crowned Wytham Ridge.

O'er the Bridge the ancient village.
Hark! The children's voices ring.
And the plough-boy whistles gaily,
While the feathered songsters sing.
Here it was I spent my boyhood,
Bright with harmless roguish fun,
Strolling round its shady Monkswood,
When my daily task was done.

Dear old Eynsham! Dear old village!
Changed indeed though you may be.
In my eyes through all the ages,
You will never change to me.
Though I'm far away, I love you,
More than that which gave me birth,
And I often tell folk, Eynsham
Is the dearest place on earth.

Eynsham Fire Brigade in the 1940s. Top row, left to right: Eric Coates, Bill Bantin, gentleman from Standlake, Peter Dormer, Perce Newport, −, −, −, −, Bill Robbins, Mons Perkins. Front row: −, 2 officers, −, Mr Tillerton, Gordy Evans.

The fire brigade's Shand-Mason horse drawn pump.

Former fireman Mons
Perkins in 1997.

Tommy Harris in June 1983
looking at a giant hogweed in his
garden. Born in 1905, Tommy has
been involved in many aspects of
village life, including the
Eynsham Carnivals and the
Parish Council. When he left
school, he went to work at
Salutation Farm by Barnard Gate.
By the time he was 19, Tommy
was working for the Oxford
building firm Kingerlee Ltd with
whom he stayed until his
retirement. He celebrated his
92nd birthday in 1997. [SC]

The lady in the middle is Mollie Harris with her son Peter taken in about 1940 in Dr Bolsover's garden. Irene Quainton is on the far right with her daughter Judith. Mollie Harris achieved local and national fame as a broadcaster and writer and played Martha Woodford in the radio show *The Archers*. She died in October 1995.

The Cope family are exceptionally talented. Kenneth (shown here) and his wife Renny both acted in the TV soap opera *Coronation Street* in the 1960s. Kenneth also co-starred as a ghost detective in the successful late 60s/early 70s show *Randall and Hopkirk (Deceased)*. Daughter Martha has already made many acting appearances on TV whilst sons Mark and Nicky are members of the successful band The Candyskins.

As well as having been a photographer for the local press, another of Sue Chapman's great achievements (seen here with the Eynsham Morris) was her involvement in the establishment of a new circular walk that was officially opened in 1994. The path starts at the southern end of station road and heads west along the old railway line. It then goes by two fields and reaches Chilbridge Road. [SC]

Sue's husband Don has been a successful journalist for the *Oxford Mail and Times* along with the *Witney Gazette.* He is shown here in 1984 with David Wastie for the occasion of a plaque being put up on the Bartholomew Room to acknowledge that in 1977 the Bartholomew Room passed into the ownership of the Parish Council. David Wastie was an Eynsham Parish Councillor for many years, being chairman for two of those. He was also president of Eynsham Football Club. Wastie Lane, the passage from Acre End Street to Back Lane was named after him. After losing his right leg in a motorcycle accident, he started up his motor repair business on the present site just off the A40 in 1951 which was then an orchard. Following his death in October 1987 aged 66, his widow Kathleen and family continued to run the business and the area now has a petrol filling station, Little Chef restaurant and the Wastie garage workshop complex. [SC]

Kathleen Wastie by Wasties Garage in 1997.

Internationally famous film director Roy Boulting came to Eynsham in the early 1990s to be near his son Rupert, who is a furniture restorer in the village, and to write his memoirs. Another of his sons is Crispian Mills lead singer with the band Kula Shaker.

Events

Weddings

The wedding of Bill Pimm and Hilda Harris held on 9 June 1930 (photo taken in the yard next to Hill House in Queen Street). Back rows, left to right: Frank Pimm, Jane Pimm, baby Frank Pimm, Andrew James Pimm, Annie Florence Pimm (née Batts), Ted Palmer, Annie Palmer (née Pimm), Tommy Harris, Charles Pimm holding Clifford Henry Pimm, Claude Hale, Leonard Pimm, Gertie Harris (who would later marry Claude Hale), Ernest Harris senior standing behind ?, Philip Pimm, June Harris, –, Mill Harris. Front row: Louisa Jane Pimm, Bertha Pimm, Edna Pimm, Doris Pimm, groom Bill Pimm, bride Hilda, Jean Harris, Frank Pimm junior, Miriam 'Midge' Harris. Frank Pimm Snr was parish clerk from 1880 until his death aged 80 in 1936.

A crowd gathers for Jack Fowler's wedding in the Square in 1935. He is remembered as a 'likeable chap' who was also a good singer.

Eynsham Carnival

Eynsham's annual carnival is usually held on the first Saturday in July and continues the tradition of its mediaeval fairs.

Eynsham Scout procession in Acre End Street before the Second World War. Amongst those marching are: Bill Harris (Scoutmaster at the front), Pete Dormer (carrying Union Jack), Jack Fowler (left of Scoutmaster), Ernie Floyd and Bert Ainsley (first and third boys behind Scoutmaster). Bert's brother Cyril played the flute in the band. Mons Perkins used to be the big drummer at the back, starting as a cub at the age of seven years in 1921. The Scouts started the carnival with the British Legion.

Fancy dress and prams, including blackened Temperance Hawtin with son Ken dressed as Topsy.

A processsion on the Queen Street/Oxford Road corner in the 1930s or 1940s.

'Mrs Archer' from the Radio 4 show The Archers making a speech at a carnival.

King George VI Coronation Celebrations, 12 May 1937

There was much carnival celebration in Eynsham for the coronation of King George VI. The Boy Scouts' Band led a procession which was judged by Dr and Mrs Tighe along with Harvey Hill. The afternoon fete was held in Mr Coates' field with activities such as children's folk dancing organised by Lottie Pimm. The children were also given Coronation mugs and ran races.

The procession in Mill Street.

A crowd at the High Street/Mill Street corner.

Some of the decorated prams. P Grant came first in the children's 'perambulators section'.

More children, fancy dress and balloons.

Other events

Post-war celebrations in the 1940s in the Coronation Crescent part of Witney Road. Amongst those included below are adults Mrs Ida Hill (at the back on the far left), Mrs Swainsbury's mother, Mrs Swainsbury, Mrs Alice Winterbourne, Mrs Rosa Green, Mrs Nash, Mrs E Harbud, Mrs N Butler-Miles, Mrs Ivy Hanks and children Beryl Bond, Mary Winterbourne, Joan Hill, Oswald Bond, Ruby Eaton, Sylvia/Christine(?) Pratley, Bill Green, Joan Winterbourne, Shirley Hanks, John Nash, Jean Nash, Bill Brown, Jean Hanks, baby Jennifer Swainsbury, — Lock.

Those included in the adults party above are Mr and Mrs H Butler-Miles, George Green (left side of the table, third person from front) and his wife, Mrs Alice Winterbourne, Mrs Keen?, Mrs Ida Hill (holding teapot), Mrs E Harbud, Mrs Swainsbury, Harvey Hill (man with parting opposite George Green), Mrs Irene Quainton (second lady down from Harvey), Mrs Ivy Hanks, Mrs Brown.

The Queen's Silver Jubilee celebrations in the Square with attendant Nicky White. For the celebrations, Wendy Smith was another attendant with Debbie Seeney as Miss Jubilee 1977. [SC]